Tattered Treasures

Tattered Treasures

STYLISH DECOR

WITH

FLEA MARKET FINDS

Lauren Powell

Sterling Publishing Co., Inc.
New York

PROLIFIC IMPRESSIONS PRODUCTION STAFF:

Editor: Mickey Baskett
Copy: Phyllis Mueller
Graphics: Dianne Miller, Karen Turpin
Styling: Mickey Baskett, Lenos Key
Photography: Jerry Mucklow
Administration: Jim Baskett

Library of Congress Cataloging-in-Publication Data Available

Published by Sterling Publishing Company, Inc.
387 Park Avenue South, New York, N.Y. 10016
Produced by Prolific Impressions, Inc.
160 South Candler St., Decatur, GA 30030
©2001 Prolific Impressions, Inc.
Distributed in Canada by Sterling Publishing
c/o Canadian Manda Group, One Atlantic Avenue, Suite 105
Toronto, Ontario, Canada M6K 3E7
Distributed in Great Britain and Europe by Cassell PLC
Wellington House, 125 Strand, London WC2R 0BB, England
Distributed in Australia by Capricorn Link (Australia) Pty. Ltd.
P.O. Box 6651, Baulkham Hills, Business Centre, NSW 2153 Australia

About the Author
Lauren Powell

Lauren Powell's background in art and design led to her interest in home decorating and her love of collecting. Her thirteen-year association with Plaid Enterprises, Inc., where she is a liaison between designers and the media, has given her extensive product knowledge in the arts and crafts field.

She has discovered many ways to update and add artistic touches to flea market finds through painted finishes, decoupage, mosaics, and more. Her home has been featured in *Woman's Day* and *Romantic Homes*, and she contributes regularly to other publications and has appeared on numerous television programs.

Lauren lives on St. Simons Island, Georgia with her husband and their two children, a Yorkshire terrier, and a thoroughbred horse. She appreciates her family's interest in her many projects and feels very blessed to have the opportunity to share her God-given talents with others.

ACKNOWLEDGEMENTS

An exciting part of writing this book was the opportunity to get to know many of the talented women among whom I live on St. Simons Island, Georgia. I would like to extend a special thank you to the following people:

This book would not have been possible without **Beverly Cavender**. Beverly opened up her wonderful home and allowed me to share many of her amazing ideas with you through this book. Her sense of style and arrangement cannot be compared. If ever visiting St. Simons Island, Georgia, be sure to check out *One of a Kind,* the truly special, you-wouldn't-want-to-miss-it antiques shop that Beverly co-owns with Melissa Bagby.

I also thank **Klickie Aiken**, a well-known real estate agent, who also allowed me to photograph her lovely home. All can learn from Klickie's eclectic mix of the old and new – collected original art, interesting architectural finds, and handpainted furniture make her home a special haven.

My special friend **Susan Driggers** is always an inspiration to me. She is an expert in the field of design and faux finishes and a constant source of encouragement to me in many ways.

Suppliers of Products
The following companies were generous in supplying me with product to use for the projects in this book. I am grateful for their readiness to help.

For sheet moss, foam sphere, handmade papers, raffia, artificial fruit, woven placemat, small seashells:
Loose ends®
P.O. Box 20310
Keizer, OR 97307

For Stencil Decor® Stencils; Stained Glass Inlay Silver Foil; Decorator Glazes, Tools, and Sealers; Royal Coat® Decoupage Medium; FolkArt® Acrylic Paints:
Plaid Enterprises, Inc.
P.O. Box 2835
Norcross, GA 30091

For slipcover and pillow patterns:
Simplicity Pattern Company, Inc.
2 Park Avenue
New York, NY 10016

For beaded trim:
Conso Products Company
2 Park Avenue
New York, NY 10016

Contents

Creating a Cozy, Lived-In Décor with Flea Market Finds

Whether it's an architectural find, an old bottle you love, an interesting basket, or even a stack of favorite books – the items you gather can work together to make a statement of your individual decorating style. By surrounding yourself with items that you find interesting and enjoyable, you will begin to create a unique, one of a kind atmosphere.

My favorite items are those that exhibit wear and age. I've discovered many beautiful treasures by simply looking beyond perfection and seeing the possibilities – in an architectural find with peeling paint, a bunch of dusty glass bottles, stacks of timeworn books, or an old suitcase. Flea markets, antique shops, even your own attic can yield rich rewards for decorating.

This book showcases these less-than-perfect "tattered treasures" and contains hundreds of examples of how to live with and display favorite flea market finds. You'll see how to create uncommon style from common objects and discover new ways to enjoy items you already own. Projects within the chapters offer ideas for using your treasures in interesting, out-of-the-ordinary ways.

The artful arrangement of books, baskets, bottles, frames, and china can turn a space into a decorator's dream. Learn to look at the things you love with an artist's eye. See things not for what they are, but what they can become – and don't take decorating too seriously.

The abundance of tag and garage sales, flea markets, and antique shows and the availability of all kinds of items on the Internet make collecting affordable and easy. I love the thrill of the hunt, especially when I'm searching for just the right item to add to a collection. As you search, I encourage you to loosen up and take a serendipitous approach. Stay on track when shopping by carrying photos of rooms and fabric swatches with you – looking at a photo of a room makes it easier to imagine an item in it, and fabric swatches help with coordinating colors.

I hope you find this book a helpful guide for displaying and appreciating the wonderful warmth and style of the tattered treasures you can collect.

Lauren Powell

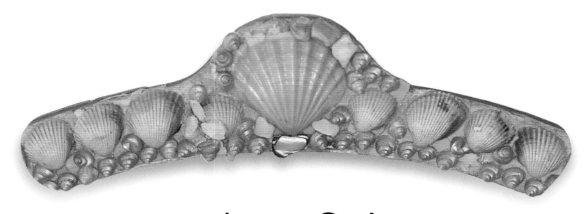

Artful Arrangements

Do you have old bottles, silverware, baskets, or books? Favorite fabrics or dishes? Arrange your treasures in groups according to color, structure, and textural interest. You may be surprised at what you have.

Groupings of similar sizes and colors work well to form collections and create balance and proportion. Look for textures and shapes that compliment each other and for height variations. Learn to look at the things you love with an artist's eye. See what you have in new ways, move things around, reposition, and blend, keeping balance in mind.

Photo at right: This concrete rooster and hen statue is most often seen in a rural setting, decorating someone's front yard. By bringing them into the house, they take on the look of an ancient sculpture, reminiscent of a country French kitchen. Their peeling paint only add to their look of authenticity.

In this living room, off-white slipcovers provide the unifying touch to unmatched upholstered sofas that showcase a medley of patterned pillows made from vintage fabrics and animal prints. Informal stacks of books are used to vary the heights of urns and boxes on the surrounding tables and invite you to relax and read. A large green plant adds a touch of the tropics; a smaller blooming plant adds color.

TIP: Deliberately understuffing the pillows, so they're not too plump, adds to the relaxed feeling. Plump pillows look more formal.

The mantelpiece is most assuredly this room's focal point. Several collections are displayed on the mantel, yet everything is arranged with balance and style and doesn't overwhelm the eye. Blue and white porcelain pieces bring color, while a variety of photographs in assorted frames adds personal touches and provides links with the past. Antique prints are framed and grouped around the mirror, which is framed in discarded tin molding. Old books stacked vertically and horizontally elevate other items.

TIP: Add height and interest by filling vases and containers with sticks, feathers, and flowers and using tall candlesticks.

TIP: Use color to create unity — china pieces in the same colors, a variety of wood and leather tones, white flowers, and white candles offer the harmony of repetition.

Cabinets and cupboards that once graced butler's pantries, breakfast rooms, and retail establishments offer space for display and storage. Here, a weathered cupboard with peeling paint holds a collection of vintage creamware and white china. Pressed glass parfait glasses hold bone and celluloid-handled vintage flatware. Herbs in clay pots share the space with a variety of vintage apothecary bottles, some of which have their original labels and contents. The cupboard doors are missing but not missed.

TIP: Outdoor items such as columns and tools give the kitchen added character.

TIP: Who knows what's in those bottles? If you're keeping the contents, be sure the bottles are sealed and kept out of the reach of small, curious children.

TIP: Consider removing doors from cabinets to better display the contents.

Old books, so plentiful at flea markets and tag sales, are a fast and inexpensive way to fill a space with color and texture. Stacked vertically or horizontally, books can cleverly elevate a lamp, show off a special vase, or fill an armoire. Collect them for their looks or their contents. (You can read them, too.)

TIP: Books look less formal if some of them are leaning. Keep books standing straight for a more formal look.

Photo at left, books in an old pine cupboard share space with a collection of porcelain dogs and wooden architectural ornaments.

Photo on this page, the display of books includes blue and white china pieces and a row of wooden finials.

Columns,
Posts
&
Architectural
Elements

Photo at right: Using architectural salvage affords the opportunity to preserve a part of history. Here, turned and carved posts make perfect candle holders. Their weathered textures and muted colors make an interesting tabletop display. Combine them with turned finials and urns for variety.

Ornamental elements from old houses and commercial buildings are often attractively weathered. Because they are easy to remove ahead of the wrecking ball, window frames and doors, with or without glass, are easy to find for sale. Here, two window frames – one arched Gothic, the other rounded Palladian – meet atop a kitchen cabinet and form the backdrop for a grouping that includes earthenware pottery, rattan-wrapped bottles, wooden spoons and bowls, and a weathered house sign.

TIP: Hang window frames and cabinet doors on the wall instead of framed art.

You can bring yesterday's architectural elegance indoors when you decorate with columns, posts, and pediment ornaments. Flanking a contemporary fireplace with a pair of weathered columns adds interest and contrasts with the texture of the stone wall.

Stools and vanity benches can be used as seating, as tables, and as footrests. Inexpensive and easy to find, their compact size allows them to fit almost anywhere. A stool with an upholstered seat offers the opportunity to display an interesting piece of fabric, too.

Photo at right: A grouping of large columns in front of a window creates plant stands of varying heights.

Turned wooden balustrades and porch spindles can be cut to any height and topped with chunky candles to create pairs of candlesticks. Two that match – or nearly match – make a pair. For color and to add the finishing touch, embellish with tassels, cords, or trims.

A wooden bowl on a pedestal showcases a seashell collection.

Architectural finds are arranged on the wall above this bed, creating a one-of-a-kind "headboard." Ornamental pieces – both wood and tin – that once graced pediments and cornices form the horizontal elements of this symmetrical grouping. Pairs of sconces and carved ornaments add to the formal arrangement.

Pillows covered with vintage floral fabrics and antique needlepoint invite you to relax.

DOORKNOB RACK

A length of weathered wood and some old doorknobs make a terrific rack for hanging coats, hats, or collectibles. Often you can find old pieces of wooden trim, shelving, or siding at salvage yards for less than a dollar. Sometimes you can get wooden planks for free! Usually doorknobs come in pairs with a metal spindle connecting them. Mix or match them as you like. How many you need depends on the length of the wood – plan to space them about 4-5" apart.

Old Doors can be so lovely that they are art in themselves. Angled in corners or placed flat against the wall, old doors and shutters add interest to nooks and crannies and can be hinged together to make screens or room dividers.

TIP: Hang a tassel from the doorknob for a touch of color.

Make-It-Yourself

WINDOW SASH PHOTO FRAME

Use a window sash to create an unusual picture frame. I took two favorite 5 x 7 color photographs to the copy shop and had them enlarged to fit.

You'll Need:
A window sash
Photocopies of photos, one for each opening in the sash, that are similar in shape to the window panes
Metal ruler
Craft knife
Mat board or posterboard
Masking tape
Sawtooth hangers *or* screw eyes and picture wire

Here's How:
1. Measure the inside openings of windows exactly. Crop the photocopies to fit, using a metal ruler and a craft knife. Place prints behind glass.
2. Cut mat board or posterboard to fit behind prints to use as a backing.
3. Position and tape backing in place with masking tape behind each print.
4. Add a sawtooth hanger or screw eyes and wire to the back of the window sash and hang on the wall. ❑

Vintage Fabrics

Vintage fabrics create a gentle look of comfort when used for draperies, upholstery, pillows, and accessories. The variety of styles, colors, and prints available offer many creative options for combining colors, periods, patterns, and prints. Vintage patterns mix well with other fabrics, antiques, and tattered treasures. Many of the fabrics were of excellent quality, allowing them to stand the test of time.

You can find vintage fabrics for sale by the piece or as yardage; purchasing drapery panels is often a good way to get larger amounts. In addition to yard goods, don't overlook old table and bed linens to use – of course – on tables or in the kitchen, bath, or bedroom or to make wonderful window valances, curtains, or pillows. Try framing a collection of embroidered handkerchiefs or pieces salvaged from a tattered quilt. A drapery panel can become a throw by sewing trim on the edges. Fringes and trims from vintage draperies can be removed and used to embellish pillows and lampshades.

Photo at right: A linen towel, embellished with embroidery and trimmed with handmade lace, is beautiful in the bathroom.

Make-It-Yourself

VINTAGE HANDKERCHIEF GIFT WRAP

Use colorful cloth hankies to make a reusable, useful giftwrap. They're perfect for a small gift, such as a piece of jewelry.

You'll Need:
A gift in a small box
A handkerchief
A piece of vintage (or other) ribbon
An old earring, clip, or other embellishment

Here's How:
1. Place the box in the center of the handkerchief. Pull up the edges around the box and gather together.
2. Tie with ribbon.
3. Clip the earring or other embellishment to the ribbon for the perfect finishing touch. ❏

TIP: Vintage fabric or wallpaper can be color copied and used as gift wrap or stationery. Or use it to cover a box for savvy storage.

This inviting chaise lounge is the ideal place to sip coffee and read the morning paper or to recline with a book after a long day. It's also a great way to display a patchwork velvet throw and a variety of pillows made from 1930s bark cloth, colonial-style toile prints, and old needlepoint. The embroidery on the tiny linen pillow in front commemorates a long-ago marriage. Old drapery fits into this decorating style. Old hatboxes piled nearby make great storage containers.

Pillows covered with vintage blue and white florals, woven damask, and ticking stripe fabrics are piled against the headboard of this bed in a guest room. Animal prints add contrast and drama and keep the look from getting too fussy.

Quality reproduction fabrics can be used to augment vintage fabrics or stand in for originals when they aren't available. Drapery departments of fabric stores stock collections of reproduction Colonial, Victorian, and 20th century floral designs. Reproduction fabrics are generally more durable and colorfast and are easier to care for than vintage fabrics. And they are available as yardage and may be as wide as 60" – an advantage if you wish to make bedcoverings or draperies without seams. There are many pillow patterns available in fabric shops for creating the variety of styles shown here.

TIP: Use old trims to adorn new fabrics.

Vintage white embroidered and ruffled cotton shams (above) are paired with black and white checks and muted-tone woven tapestry pillows to give this bed a decorator touch. Tassels and trims add contrast.

Designer Deb Burns loves to combine a variety of vintage fabrics and reproduction fabrics to create one-of-a-kind upholstery and slipcovers. She chooses harmonizing colors and different-scale prints to create pleasing combinations. This approach is a great solution for active families – it's easy to replace sections that get torn or stained – and a wonderful way to use fabrics in good condition when you don't have sufficient yardage to cover an entire piece of furniture.

Make-It-Yourself

FRAMED VINTAGE DRESSER SCARF

Designed by Ann Barnes

One way to preserve special linens and keepsakes is to frame them. A piece of handmade paper was chosen as the background to accentuate the bold yellow stitching on this piece. When framing precious textiles, use Plexiglas, which allows the fabric to breathe and blocks destructive light, instead of glass and use acid-free mat boards and papers.

You'll Need:

A frame with glass or Plexiglas to fit

A vintage dresser, scarf, towel, napkin, or handkerchief

Mat board

Craft knife

Handmade paper

Needle and thread

Wire brads

Masking tape

Awl or ice pick

Here's How:

1. Cut mat board to fit frame. Position handmade paper on mat board.

2. Arrange fabric piece on handmade paper, choosing an arrangement that shows the best parts of the piece and hides any flaws.

3. With a needle and thread, tack fabric to handmade paper and mat board. Use an awl or ice pick to make holes in the mat board. Tie ends of thread at back to secure.

4. Place mat board with paper and fabric piece attached in frame.

5. Secure with wire brads at edges. Tape over edges to secure and keep out dust. ❑

Make-It-Yourself

VINTAGE FABRIC-LINED BASKET

Add a colorful accent to a room and keep things neat and tidy in a vintage fabric lined basket. It's a great way to use a treasured small piece of a favorite fabric. It will also add a feminine touch of indulgence to a plain inexpensive basket.

You'll Need:
Fabric
Basket
Chalk or disappearing fabric
    marker
Elastic, 1/4" wide
Needle and thread

Here's How:
1. Place basket upside down on wrong side of fabric. Measure depth of basket and add 2". Use ruler to measure out this amount from edge of basket. Mark cutting line with chalk or a disappearing marker, following basket shape (round, rectangular, etc.).
2. Cut out fabric.
3. Fold under cut edge of fabric to form a casing and sew leaving an opening for inserting the elastic.
4. Cut a length of elastic 1/2" smaller than the circumference of the basket. Insert elastic in casing.
5. Stitch elastic together at ends. Stitch opening of fabric casing closed.
6. Place fabric in basket and slip elastic over the edge to hold in place. ❏

Furniture
and
Fixtures

Weather and wear impart the patina of time
to painted wood, wicker, and metal surfaces, giving
them a unique beauty. Sometimes a piece is just
perfect as is; other times refurbishing is in order.
Using the variety of do-it-yourself products
available, it's possible to create aged and distressed
finishes that rival Mother Nature's.
Reupholstering or adding a slipcover can
work wonders on chairs or sofas that have seen
better days.

Photo at right: Adding a weathered cabinet to a room to display a collection of dishes, tools, and baskets instantly adds architectural interest and age to a new house.

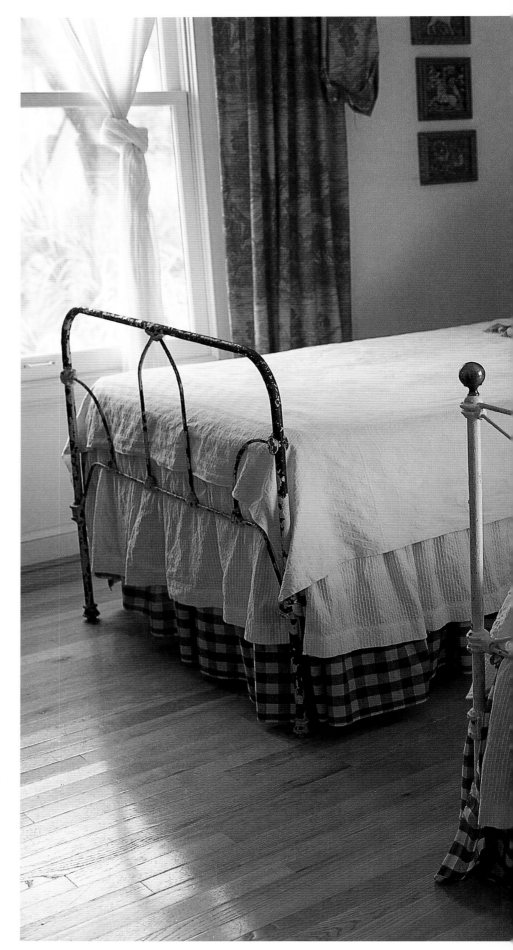

Sometimes a room is more interesting when the pieces of a "pair" do not match exactly. Here, mismatched iron-frame twin beds are unified by gingham dust ruffles and similar white vintage bed linen coverlets.

Old wicker adds charm and texture to any room. Although easy to refurbish with spray paint, the look of natural aging on wicker is hard to duplicate. I enjoy a rubbed off painted finish that highlights the lovely texture.

TIP: Not using seat cushions or back cushions shows off wicker's woven beauty.

HOW TO CREATE CRACKLED FINISHES

What normally takes years of wind and weather can be created on painted surfaces instantly with a crackle medium, which is sold at paint, crafts, and hardware stores.

I like the technique called "one-color crackle." The surface is painted with white or cream paint and allowed to dry. Crackle medium is brushed over the paint in long, smooth strokes. When the crackle medium is dry, a topcoat of waterbase varnish is applied. The finish will begin to crackle as the varnish dries. When the varnish is dry, an antiquing glaze is rubbed over the surface to reveal the cracks.

The "two-color crackle" technique uses a topcoat in a contrasting paint color. The underneath color will be revealed when the top coat color dries.

A thicker topcoat creates bigger cracks; a thinner topcoat creates finer, smaller cracks. **Don't** overbrush.

This photo shows antiquing the "one-color crackle" technique. The surface was painted gray, then a coat of crackle medium was added. When crackle medium was dry, a coat of varnish was applied. Cracks then formed. When varnish was dry, brown antiquing was applied.

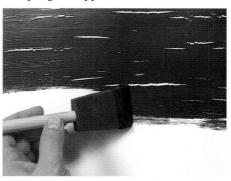

This photo shows the "two-color crackle" technique. The surface was painted white. When paint was dry, crackle medium was applied. When medium was dry, black paint was applied. Cracks formed in the top layer as it dried, revealing the white first coat.

Photo at left: Weather and wear have aged and mellowed this painted cabinet. To duplicate the look, sand wood and wipe away dust. Apply crackle medium and let dry. Apply a topcoat of white paint (cracks will form instantly.) Let dry. Sand the edges for a worn look and scrape the paint away in spots. Vacuum up dust and paint chips. Rub with a brown-tone antiquing medium or glaze mixture. Let dry.

Cabinets don't have to be white – although many of the old ones you're likely to find will be. The colorful cabinet, *pictured at right,* that was first used in a post office for sorting mail, is the focal point of this European-inspired kitchen. Now it showcases the owner's pottery and collectibles. The antiqued green and salmon colors on this cabinet work wonderfully with the room's aged yellow walls.

Pictured below: This antique folding campaign table, is perfect for serving appetizers or dessert in the living room. It can be set up anywhere, is easily stored when not in use, and takes up little space in a room. Unique pieces like this are not easily found. When you spot one – buy it – then figure out how to use it later.

HOW TO PAINT & ANTIQUE

Any wooden furniture or cabinetry piece can become a one-of-a-kind painted treasure. Your own attic, basement, or garage may hold a piece of furniture that would be suitable for a painted finish.

When choosing an old piece of furniture to paint, consider the style, shape, and function of the piece when deciding what to do. Be sure the piece is in sound condition. If it needs regluing or other work, have repairs made before you paint.

When you are preparing and painting the piece, be sure to work in a well-ventilated area and wear gloves and a dust mask. Stripping is necessary if old, peeling paint and varnish can't be sanded smooth or if you want to apply a finish that will show the wood grain. You can take it to a professional or do it yourself. If you decide to strip the piece yourself, choose a stripping agent that is nontoxic and odor free and follow the manufacturer's instructions regarding use, disposal, and protective equipment needed.

You'll Need:
A piece of furniture
Cloth rags
Cleanser (see Step 1)
Sandpaper, 150 and 220 grit
Tack cloth for wiping up sanding dust
Spackling compound *or* stainable latex wood filler
Satin acrylic paint
Neutral glazing medium and brown colored glaze *or* premixed waterbase antiquing medium
Acrylic varnish
Paint brush
Sponge and rags for applying antiquing medium or glaze
Options: Primer, old toothbrush and palette knife for spattering

Here's How:
1. Remove hardware. Clean the surface. What you need to do depends on the condition of the piece; at the very least, wipe the piece with a damp cloth to remove all dust and debris. You'll need to remove all wax, grease, or furniture polish with cleanser, rubbing alcohol, a liquid sandpaper product, or mineral spirits.
2. Sand lightly to smooth. Wipe away dust.
3. *If you're painting the piece,* use spackling compound to fill unwanted dents, cracks, and holes, let dry, and sand. *If you're applying a finish that will show the wood grain,* such as a transparent stain, apply a neutral color stainable latex filler, remove excess while wet, and allow to dry. Sand smooth. If the filler has shrunk during drying, apply more filler, let dry, and sand.
4. **Optional:** *If you're painting the piece,* apply primer. Let dry. Sand. Wipe away dust. **Don't** use primer if you're applying a finish that will show the wood grain.
5. Paint with satin finish acrylic paint. (The satin finish of the paint allows the glaze to glide on smoothly.) Let dry.
6. Create a glaze mixture with brown colored glaze + a neutral glazing medium or use a premixed waterbase antiquing medium. Apply lightly with a damp kitchen sponge. Rub in the direction of the wood grain to remove excess glaze. Let dry.
7. **Optional:** Thin glaze mixture or antiquing medium with water. Spatter surface by loading an old toothbrush with the thinned glaze or medium. Hold the brush over the surface and run your thumb or a palette knife over the bristles. (The size of the spatters is determined by the consistency of the glaze; a more watery mixture makes smaller spatters. Test on a piece of paper before spattering your project.) Let dry.
8. Apply a topcoat of acrylic varnish.
9. Clean and replace hardware. ❑

A CABINET THAT TELLS A STORY

The cabinet in the photo at right is adorned with a passage from one of my most-loved books, Black Beauty.

You'll Need:
Basic Supplies listed in "How to Paint & Antique," above, plus:
A permanent marker
Posterboard, for practicing
Straight edge and pencil
Spray-on varnish compatible with acrylic paint

Here's How:
1. Prepare, paint, and antique your furniture piece, following the "How to Paint & Antique" instructions above, Steps 1 through 6.
2. Choose the words you wish to include, such as poetry, lines from a favorite book, or Bible verses. Practice writing with a permanent marker on a piece of posterboard cut to the size of the furniture to test your spacing. Draw lines to guide you if you need them.
3. When you're satisfied with the look, draw light pencil lines to guide you and use the marker to write the words on the furniture.
4. Seal with a spray-on varnish. Let dry.
5. Replace hardware. ❑

The first place I can w[ell]
pleasant meadow with
it. Some shady trees leaned
water lilies grew at the de[ep]
One side we looked int[o]
the other we looked ove[r]
use, which stood by th[e]
the meadow was a pl[ant]
the bottom there was [a]
overhung by a steep ban[k]
lived upon my mother's[-]
grass. In the daytime I
night I lay down close
we used to stand by
the trees, and when it wa[s]
warm shed near the p[lantation]
old enough to eat grass[,]
work in the daytime an[d]
ing. There were six you[ng]
besides me. They were
were nearly as large
ran with them and
ed to gallop all togeth[er]
the field, as hard as we
had rather rough play[,]
d frequently bite and k[ick]
a day when there was a
mother whinnied to me
she said, "I wish you to

I remember was a large
a pond of clear water in
over it, and rushes and
ep end. Over the hedge on
a plowed field, and on
a gate. at our master's ho[use]
roadside. At the top of
a[ ]ion of fir trees, and at
[sof]tly running brook
k. While I was young I
milk, as I could not eat
ran by her side, and at
by her. When it was hot,
the pond in the shade of
s cold, we had a nice
plantation. As soon as I was
my mother went out to
d came back in the even
ng colts in the meadow
older than I was; some
as grown up horses. I
had great fun. We us
er round and round
could go. Sometimes we
for the older colts wou[ld]
ick as well as gallop. On[e]
good deal of kicking, my
to come to her, and then
pay attention to what I

| Make-It-Yourself |

PAINTING DIAMONDS

This plain piece of furniture was given some pizzazz by adding dramatic diamonds to the front and sides. Masking tape is the essential tool used to create the diamond effect. The size of the doors determines the size and shape of the diamonds.

You'll Need:
Basic Supplies listed in "How to Paint & Antique," above, plus:
Straight edge and pencil
Acrylic satin paint in a second color

Here's How:
1. Prepare, paint, and antique your furniture piece, following the "How to Paint & Antique" instructions above, Steps 1 through 5.
2. Close the doors. On one door only, use a straight edge to connect the top left corner to the bottom right corner. With a pencil, lightly mark the line from corner to corner. Repeat the same procedure from top right corner to bottom left corner. Repeat on other door to complete a pencil line pattern to form the diamond shapes.
3. Mask off center diamond with low-tack masking tape. Paint the diamond. Remove tape. Let dry 24 hours.
4. Mask off remaining side half-diamond shapes. Paint. Remove tape. Let dry completely.
5. Antique the entire piece, following instructions in Step 6, "How to Paint & Antique."
6. Seal with varnish. ❏

Taping off diamond shapes.

TIP: Changing hardware on a piece of furniture dramatically changes the look.

Make-It-Yourself

HOW TO CREATE DISTRESSED FINISHES

Distressed finishes look comfortably worn. You can create this look of age and wear by applying wax to some areas of a surface before painting or applying wax between layers of paint. In areas where wax has been applied, the paint is easy to remove.

Distressed furniture doesn't need a protective finish; after all, if it becomes more distressed, it should not matter. But you may choose to seal tabletops from ring marks or food stains with matte varnish.

You'll Need:

Acrylic paint, one or more colors

Clear or white candle or canning wax (paraffin), sold at grocery and hardware stores (Do not use colored candles – the dye could stain your project.)

Paint brushes

Tools for distressing (choose one or two): a butter knife, paint scraper, putty knife or tin can lid, an ice pick, a piece of chain, or a hammer

Sandpaper, 220 grit

Antiquing glaze

Photo 1

Here's How:

1. Apply wax to surface with the grain of the wood, concentrating the wax in areas where paint would most likely be worn away by handling, such as edges. If you're using a base paint, apply 1-3 coats of the base color and let dry, then apply the wax. *See photo 1.*
2. Apply 1-3 coats of paint. The paint coats can be the same color or different colors. Let dry between coats but **do not** sand between coats. Let dry.
3. Scrape surface with the tool of your choice, working in the direction of the wood grain, to reveal the raw wood or base paint or both. In areas where wax was applied, paint will flake off easily. Brush away the paint particles as you scrape. *See photo 2.*
4. Sand surface to smooth areas where paint has been removed. Use sanding pads or sandpaper wrapped around a block of wood on flat areas. On curved areas, wrap the sandpaper around your index finger. In tight, straight areas, fold the sandpaper a few times to create a thickness that fits the area.
5. For a layered effect, use two or more paint colors. Allow paint to dry between colors and rub the wax over the painted surface before adding the next color. When all paint colors are applied and dry and the surface is scraped, the layers of paint will be exposed.
6. Use an antiquing glaze to mellow the effect. Purchase an antiquing glaze and paint it over the piece. For a more subtle look, antiquing glaze can be wiped off while still wet, allowing it to concentrate in grooves and low areas.

Photo 2

These pine paneled cabinets, *at right,* were painted with a mustard color and antiqued and spattered with brown for a mellow, aged look. They were formerly knotty pine; the new finish gives them an updated European look.

Photo at left: This shows the progression of the finish that was created on these kitchen cabinets. *From left to right:* Base paint color was a soft mustard yellow; the middle section shows base paint with brown antiquing glaze added; the far right section shows base paint + antiquing + spattering.

Many interesting pieces of upholstered furniture can be found at flea markets and garage sales, and comfortable favorites can be updated and given new life through reupholstering or slipcovering.

When choosing a piece to reupholster, consider the overall style and whether the frame is in good condition. If you like the basic lines of the furniture, and the price is right, go ahead and buy it! Several yards of fabric later, you'll have something truly customized for you.

These chairs from the 1950s, *at right,* were reupholstered in vibrant red, and their exposed wooden legs were painted black. When purchasing a chair you plan to use for seating, be sure the chair is strong and stable enough to hold the weight of an adult. If repairs are needed, have them made before reupholstering. If the chair is really wobbly and can't be repaired, place it where no one can sit in it and use it for decoration only.

TIP: To really enhance and change a piece, paint exposed wood in contrasting colors.

Don't automatically assume you need to reupholster – a slipcover may be just what's needed to refresh the look or change the color of a chair. Slipcover patterns are available in many different styles, and slipcovers are easy to make, even for beginners.

Shown in these photos are two chair styles and an arm treatment closeup. The lines of the pieces were wonderful and they were structurally sound, yet the fabric was worn and dirty. Slip covers add a fresh comfortable look.

Wooden Chairs

Chairs are a functional collectible. Painted, reupholstered, or left as is, wooden chairs can be used for seating or as accessories for any room – they can even become a piece of art. Folded towels look great stacked on a chair in the bathroom. A tiny chair on a table can become a plant stand or a surface for display.

Photo at right: A collection of miniature chairs decorates the wall of this powder room. The unevenly glazed walls provide a rustic background.

Place a small wooden chair on top of a dresser to hold a pillow, plant, frame, or other accessory. It's a great way to showcase a treasured child-size chair and elevate it to a work of art.

This wooden chair displays an antique christening gown that's draped over the back. Sunlight streaming from a window illuminates the gown and the chair's shape.

A salvaged painted chair, *above,* adds a delightful and important touch of color to the garden. A chair that's not sturdy enough to sit in can be useful as a plant stand.

A wooden chair without a seat, *right,* is placed on top of an armoire. The chair holds a basket that holds a pot of trailing ivy.

Make-It-Yourself

PAINTING AN OLD CHAIR

Painting is an inexpensive, easy way to completely change the look of an old chair and create an eye-catching accent piece. An upholstered seat can easily be re-covered in a coordinating or contrasting fabric for a fresh new look.

You'll Need:
A chair
Acrylic satin paint
Neutral glazing medium and brown colored glaze
  or premixed waterbase antiquing medium
Fabric in a coordinating color
Sandpaper
Tack cloth
Paint brush
Staple gun and staples

Here's How:
1. Remove the seat from the chair. Sand the chair smooth. Wipe away dust with a tack cloth.

2. Paint the chair with two coats of acrylic paint. Let dry and sand lightly between coats.

3. Mix colored transparent glaze + neutral glazing medium to make an antiquing glaze. Apply glaze mixture with a brush. Wipe away excess, allowing glaze to settle in cracks and crevices. Let dry.

4. Cover the seat with fabric, securing fabric with staples. Replace seat. ❏

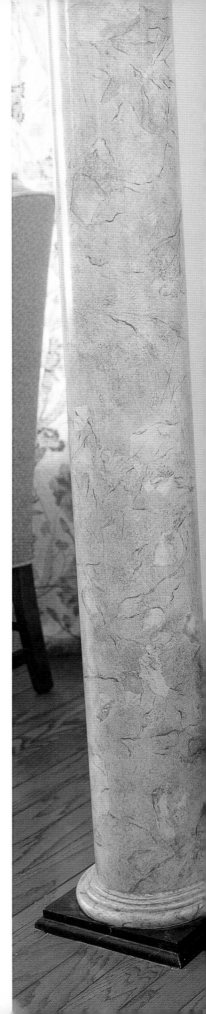

China
Collections

Years ago, for a few dollars, I bought my first antique plate and proudly displayed it on a stand. Today I still am drawn to beautiful china. The wide array of colors, designs, patterns, and motifs available make collecting china fun and interesting, and I enjoy using mismatched china to create unusual place settings.

Used as an accessory, a piece of china can fit any decor style. Displayed as art, several pieces hung on a wall add dimensional interest. Pieces can be combined by common colors or themes.

Don't pass up broken, chipped, or cracked china. These pieces can be bought at minimum prices and used in many creative ways. You can use old bowls, pitchers, and soup tureens to hold flowers and greenery. Sometimes I buy inexpensive patterned pieces with the intent of breaking them for mosaic projects.

Don't toss broken pieces of china. Collect broken shards and use them to fill a bowl, *right,* for a stunning centerpiece on the dining room table.

Mounted to a wall, *below,* blue and white china plates and surviving lids from long-broken soup tureens create textural contrast on blue and white shell-patterned wallpaper. The positioning of the pieces creates symmetrical balance around the carved-frame mirror.

The natural crackling that occurs in the glazes of old ironstone and china adds to the vintage charm. I enjoy mixing creamware pieces with printed patterns and pastel solids.

The painted cabinet, *pictured above and at right,* holds a collection of china pieces and glass-domed metal cake stands. The beadboard backing was added to the cabinet and stained with a blue gray glaze for subtle contrast.

A china collection can be organized around a pattern, a color, a style, a vintage, or a theme. A collection of china in various floral patterns and solid dove blue, *below,* fills an antique china cabinet.

The collector of this assortment, *right,* chose violets as the theme for her collection. She has augmented the colorful violet-patterned china with deep green and solid dove blue pieces. Notice the variety of violet patterns – even though the actual designs are different, the color and theme ties the collection together. What a beautiful table this create for a spring luncheon or brunch; or a special bridal tea.

FRAMING A CHINA PLATE

Framing can make a special piece of art out of an odd china plate you don't plan to use for serving. I found the frame at a flea market. This a good way to use a frame whose glass has broken because you don't need the glass.

You'll Need:
A frame
Mat board
Sheet moss
White craft glue
Epoxy glue *or* glue gun and glue sticks

Here's How:
1. Measure the opening. Cut a piece of mat board to fit the size of the opening.
2. Glue sheet moss to the mat board with white craft glue. Let dry.
3. Use epoxy or hot glue to glue the moss covered mat board in the frame opening.
4. Glue the plate at center as shown, using epoxy or hot glue. ❏

MAKING CHINA SHARD JEWELRY

Broken pieces of decorated china can make show-stopping jewelry. By adding trims, tassels, beads, pearls, or other ornamental elements from vintage or costume jewelry to china shards, you can make wonderful wearable art. Use emery cloth to smooth the edges and a jewelry glue to adhere trims. The copper or silver foil-backed tapes that are used to make stained glass are another good choice for covering the edges. Add additional embellishments of your choice and finish with a pin back.

Make-It-Yourself

CHINA SHARD MOSAIC TABLE

Designed by Sandra McCooey

A mosaic table is a wonderful way to preserve a treasured broken piece of china. Combine broken pieces and chips of china with tiles to form a tabletop everyone in the family can enjoy. If necessary, break the china in smaller pieces by laying a towel over the piece and gently tapping with a hammer.

You'll Need:
A table
Broken china pieces and tiles,
   enough to cover the top
White craft glue or tile adhesive
Sandpaper, 150 grit
Sanded grout

Here's How:
1. Sand the surface of the table. Wipe away dust.
2. Glue flat pieces of broken china to tabletop. Fill in gaps with small tiles. Let dry.
3. Mix sanded grout and apply according to the manufacturer's instructions. ❏

TIP: To keep the configuration of a plate, lay plate on contact paper, cover with a towel, and gently tap with a hammer. This will keep pieces together and make it easier to reconstruct the plate when you glue it on the table.

TIP: Paint the table legs to coordinate with the china colors for a dramatic effect.

Make-It-Yourself

CHINA SHARD TOPIARY

The natural mossy texture combined with brightly colored china adds a touch of whimsy to a screened porch or sun-room. Begin by collecting flat pieces of broken china, or lay plates inside a folded towel and break with a hammer into small and medium size pieces.

You'll Need:
Pieces of broken china
Green floral foam sphere
Sheet moss
White craft glue
Optional: Finial or architectural
   ornament

Here's How:
1. Glue china to sphere, leaving some space between the pieces.

2. Tear sheet moss in pieces. Glue moss to fill spaces between china shards.

3. Place sphere on a metal stand or on a column or other architectural element.

4. *Option:* Glue a finial or architectural ornament on top. ❏

Glass Bottles & Jars

Old glass bottles and jars make excellent containers for all kinds of common household products – the range of shapes and sizes available allows unmeasured creativity.

Photo at right, A wine bottle with beautiful etching becomes a lovely bottle for holding dishwashing detergent conveniently next to the sink. It is much prettier than those plastic squeeze bottles, and is uncommonly indulgent. The bright red tomato juice can used to hold cut flowers adds a touch of pop art to brighten this space.

Bath oils and bubble bath take on sophisticated elegance when stored in glass bottles and displayed in the bathroom. (Use corks to seal them if lids can't be found.) Salt and sugar shakers can hold bath salts and powders.

TIP: Personalized bottles make great gifts. Paints specifically designed for use on glass are available at crafts and hobby stores.

The dainty floral design painted on this bottle is lovely in the bathroom.

Old glass bottles and jars that can stand up to vigorous scrubbing can be used to store food and condiments. Or, transfer herbs and spices from store-bought tins, jars, or bags into recycled vintage bottles. Buy some pre-printed self-stick labels or create your own on a copy machine or computer.

These antique apothecary bottles, *below,* hold what remains of a long-forgotten agricultural display.

The warmth of an Italian kitchen inspired this combination, *right,* of rattan wrapped bottles, golden glazed pottery, and bread boards on an old farm table.

Make-It-Yourself

MESSAGE IN A BOTTLE

Sneak a peek inside this old canning jar with a zinc lid to see a postcard from the early 1900s. A jar is a great way to preserve a piece of history. A bit of dried moss covers the bottom of the jar, and the postcard fits snugly inside. The jar lid is tied with a natural raffia bow.

Use your imagination and add a splash of color to any area, indoors or out. Put blooms on any tree with hanging vases made from old bottles. Simply wrap thin wire around the bottle's neck and attach the end of the wire to a tree branch. Fill bottles with water and blooming flowers. Use the same technique to add colorful blooms on a deck railing.

Collectible Containers

Unusual containers can hold keys, important papers, kitchen utensils, fruits, books, vegetables, or nothing at all! Trays, buckets, bowls, baskets, and suitcases are some of my favorites.

Photo at right: Antique woven baskets with handles are hung from a metal millinery stand that once held hats in a department store.

Collectible Containers

A china bowl, *right,* holds an assortment of tea bags on a kitchen counter. A piece of marble extracted from a Victorian wash stand is beautiful atop this kitchen counter and serves as a great working surface.

Baskets of uniform size, *below,* organize a variety of items on open shelves in this kitchen cabinet.

Vintage luggage, *opposite,* provides storage while creating an atmosphere that is reminiscent of a romantic tropical resort – the kind Hemmingway or Humphrey Bogart would have visited. In this den, the larger suitcase stores sheets near the sleeper sofa to make up the bed for an overnight guest. The train case nearby holds a towel, washcloth, soap, and toiletries.

Make-It-Yourself

EMBELLISHED BASKET

This inexpensive, yard sale basket was embellished with metallic beaded trim, which changed its look and style. Colorful imitation fruit fills the basket and never spoils.

You'll Need:
A basket
Metallic beaded trim
Sheet moss
White craft glue
Trim of your choice

Here's How:

1. Cut sheet moss to fit bottom of basket. Glue in place.

2. Glue trim around outside of basket under upper edge. ❏

A tin paint bucket, left outdoors, will naturally rust and age. I enjoy using these containers for plants in the garden. Put a clay or plastic pot inside and fill around the top of the pot with moss.

Frames, Prints & Photos

Old frames are a lovely way to show off photos, keepsakes, and collectibles, and the frames themselves can be as interesting as their contents. From painted and peeling to gilded gold or decorated with buttons, beads, and seashells, frames make powerful decorating statements.

A grouping of frames in similar styles can create a mood. Vintage jewelry, beads, and baubles give a feminine feeling. Peeling paint evokes a country look. Using the same type of frame can lend unity to a group of photos or prints. Conversely, groupings of similar subjects can unify disparate frames. I love to vary the heights of my collections and display several frames together on a bedside table.

Photo at right, a treasured photograph is displayed in a frame ornamented with vintage buttons and bits of old costume jewelry – odd earrings and a broken strand of beads. Jewelry glue was used to attach the vintage jewelry.

Shelves added to an old ornate frame create a shadow box for displaying a rather formal collection of tiny treasures. To make a shadow box, build a box with shelves to fit your frame and glue to the frame's back edge. Add a backing on the box or let the wall show as it does here.

A tiny bell jar, *below,* holds a treasured photo, a pocket watch, and other memorabilia.

A collection of antique frames on a table, *right,* is a lovely way to display family photos.

Make-It-Yourself

CORK PHOTO FRAME

This intriguing frame is made from wine corks with printed designs. As the base, you could use a frame made from wooden molding or a flat acrylic pocket frame. Embellish with a raffia bow and a cluster of artificial grapes and greenery. It's quick, easy, and fun.

Make-It-Yourself

FRAMED CORKBOARD

Keep favorite mementos in view on a corkboard. I use mine for favorite fabric swatches, special letters and drawings from my children, postcards from traveling friends, and reminder notes.

You'll Need:

Frame (size of your choice)

Cork sheet to fit the frame (find it at crafts and
  hardware stores)

Ruler

Craft knife

Heavy-duty glue

Here's How:

1. Measure the inside opening of the frame.
2. Cut cork to fit the opening with a craft knife.
3. Glue cork to inside lip of frame using heavy duty
   glue. ❑

Create unified groupings by choosing subjects with similar themes, similar frames, or mats in the same color. Framed magazine covers from earlier decades make interesting conversation pieces. The antique *House Beautiful* magazine covers, *above,* have the same frames and same color mats.

A grouping of old botanical prints, *right,* are framed with a variety of inexpensive, narrow wooden frames. Unified by subject, they are far more interesting and eye-catching because they are hung together

TIP: Use old prints and photos to create decoupage projects. Photocopy the originals on a color photocopier and use the copies for projects.

Frames, Prints & Photos

Special letters and photos hold a dear place in our hearts. Rather than hiding them away, frame them and enjoy them year round as shown below.

Black and white family photos in simple frames, *right,* are hung close together on the paneled wall of a den – a much better way to enjoy them than keeping them in an album. If you're thinking about hanging old photos in a sunny room, consider having copies made and safely storing your irreplaceable originals.

Make-It-Yourself

FRAMED BLACKBOARD

Create a blackboard from an old frame and have fun leaving special notes for family members.

You'll Need:
A frame
Thin plywood
Blackboard paint
Glue or wire brads
Paint brush

Here's How:
1. Measure the inside opening of the frame.
2. Cut a piece of thin plywood to fit the opening.
3. Paint plywood with blackboard paint. Let dry.
4. Glue in place or attach to frame with wire brads. ❑

Make-It-Yourself

DECOUPAGED LUGGAGE

This simple cut-and-paste technique can be used to adorn all kinds of surfaces. Shapes are cut from prints, cards, or other paper or fabric and adhered to the surface with decoupage medium. Several coats of decoupage medium are brushed on to seal.

A falling-apart 1897 copy of Black Beauty was the inspiration for this decoupage project. Old pages and pictures were torn from the book and randomly applied.

You'll Need:
Pages (or photocopies of pages) from an old book
A suitcase
Black paint
Paint brush
Decoupage medium
Sandpaper, 400 grit

Here's How:
1. Paint the suitcase with black paint. Let dry.
2. Use sandpaper to remove the black base paint in areas to mimic an aged finish. Wipe away dust.
3. Cut out pages or parts of pages from the book or photocopies.
4. Brush backs of prints with decoupage medium. Position and press to surface, smoothing them with your fingers. Let dry.
5. Brush several coats of decoupage medium over the suitcase to seal. ❑

TIP: Use color photocopies instead of originals. The thinner photocopy paper is easy to work with, and you can keep your originals intact.

Metalwork

The intricate details on old cast ironwork and the
sturdy simplicity of hand-forged pieces are
wonderful to look at and can be used indoors and
out. Functional pieces should be protected from
rust with sealer or paint so they will stay strong and
stable; however, on decorative pieces, a rusted or
patina finish is often most desirable.

I love the characteristic weathering that takes
place on iron and tin left outdoors – the rusted
surface is both charming and appealing. To achieve
a rusted look, you'll need to remove any paint or
sealer that has been applied to a piece. The "naked"
iron will rust naturally when left outside.

Photo at right: This stylized metal shore bird once decorated a
screen door. Now it's the focal point on a lattice-lined porch.

Iron brackets with leaves and scrolls frame a window, *below,* over a kitchen sink. Iron and metal are also great in the bathroom – the moisture only adds to their appeal.

A cast iron fireplace screen, *right,* is hung on a bathroom wall. A metal filigree piece holds jewelry and a tall stand holds a candle.

Make-It-Yourself
STENCILED FIREPLACE SCREEN

A pre-cut stencil design was used to embellish this iron mesh fireplace screen.

You'll Need:

A fireplace screen
A pre-cut stencil
Low tack masking tape
A measuring tape
A stencil brush

Acrylic craft paint in a light color
Disposable plate or palette
Drop cloths or layers of newspaper
Paper towels

Here's How:

1. Prepare your work area by laying out a drop cloth or layers of newspaper.
2. Center the stencil motif on the center panel of the screen and tape in place.
3. Pour a small puddle of paint on a disposable plate or palette.
4. Dip the tips of the stencil brush in the paint and blot the brush on paper towels to remove most of the paint.
5. Apply paint lightly through the openings of the stencil, using a circular motion. Remove stencil. Let dry. ❑

Old institutional-size muffin tins become a backsplash and add interest to the wall space between the countertop and cabinets in this kitchen. A tomato juice can holds flowers, and a red tin bucket holds a roll of paper towels.

Lamps

Lamps can be both decorative and functional.
I enjoy having unique lamps and have discovered
that many items can easily be made into lamps.
(This is a good lesson in seeing beyond the
original purpose of an item.) Vases, statues, baskets,
teapots – all types of unique containers – can
be easily transformed into one-of-a-kind
lighting accessories with parts you can buy at
the hardware store.

TIP: Take the lamp base with you
when you choose a shade.

Photo at right: A seashell assortment spills out of the base of this
bamboo lamp. The shade is a wire frame covered with jute
twine. A seashell finial provides a finishing touch.

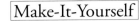

FABRIC COVERING FOR A LAMP

Fabric covers the pole and the shade of this lamp – updating the look and making it fit with a particular decorating scheme.

You'll Need:

A pole lamp with a lampshade
Fabric
Elastic, 1/4" wide
Needle and thread
Scissors
Iron and ironing board
Ribbon or cording
White craft glue

Here's How:

1. Remove light bulb socket from lamp.
2. Measure the height and circumference of the pole of the lamp. Cut a piece of fabric as wide as the circumference measurement plus 1" and as long as two times the height measured plus 1".
3. Fold fabric in half lengthwise, wrong sides together, and sew a seam. Turn and press.
4. Slip fabric tube over the pole, gathering it along the pole.
5. Replace light bulb socket.
6. Secure fabric at top of pole with a spot of glue. Tie ribbon around top of pole over fabric.
7. Measure the circumference of the bottom of the lampshade and the height of the lampshade.
8. Cut a piece of fabric as wide as the circumference of the bottom of the shade plus 1" and as long as the height plus 2".
9. Fold top edge under 1/2" to form a casing. Cut a piece of elastic as long as the circumference of the top of the lampshade. Insert elastic into casing, gather fabric on elastic, and stitch ends of elastic together.
10. Hem bottom. Slip fabric covering over lampshade. ❑

A tiskit, a tasket, a lamp made from a basket! In a kitchen, bedroom, or study, this basket lamp brightens up a corner or other small space. The old, stained paper shade was covered with a vintage fabric by simply gluing the fabric to the paper shade.

A collectible tin can container can be drilled, wired, and used as an attractive base for a lamp. This decorated tin was mounted on a wooden base, fitted with lamp hardware, and topped with a pleated fabric shade.

TIP: To make a lamp, some items may require drilling. Many home improvement stores have someone who can do this for you.

117

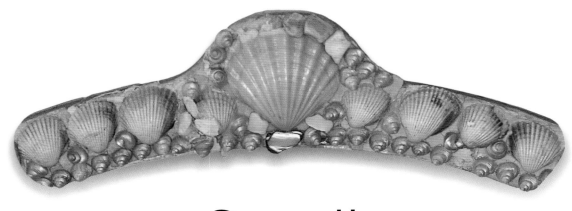

Small Collections

You may already be a collector and not even realize it. Look around your own home for similar items – many times we scatter things throughout the house instead of displaying them together as a collection. Search attics and closets, and look at what you already have. Bring heirlooms and sentimental favorites out of storage to enjoy.

Photo at right: Seashells take center stage when displayed in an elegant old urn.

Display similar items
together to create a collection.
These vintage cameras, with
their various shapes and
detailed workmanship, make
an interesting arrangement
below a wall of framed black
and white photographs.

Collect corks from dinner parties and favorite restaurant meals and display them in a bowl, *below*. For lasting memories, write dates and the names of your dinner companions on them.

A collection of corkscrews looks great displayed on a tabletop with a tray of decanters, *right*.

Because we live by the ocean, my family is always collecting seashells. Who can resist their wonderful shapes and colors? Create an instant centerpiece for the table by filling urns, baskets, and bowls with your collection. Add some small shovels for building metaphorical sand castles.

Small seashells can be glued on boxes and frames for storage or as an unusual giftwrap. Here, they cover a paperboard box.

Gather your trophies and urns – polish them till they sparkle. Fill them with flowers in the summer. The different sizes make the display more interesting. Carol Holloway's trophy collection inspired me to create this stacked display.

Make-It-Yourself

SERVING TRAY WITH BENT SPOON HANDLES

Old flatware – silver, plated, and stainless – can be used for dining or creatively recycled to create functional accessories.
Created by Susan Goans-Driggers

You'll Need:
An oval wooden plaque
2 tablespoons
Sandpaper
Tack cloth
Paint or stain (I used a patina verdigris faux finish paint kit for this)
Paint brushes and/or sponges
Drill with drill bits and screw attachment
Screws
Felt self-stick pads

Here's How:
1. Sand wooden surface smooth. Wipe away dust with a tack cloth.
2. Bend the handles of the spoons with pliers, using photo as a guide.
3. Drill holes in the bowls of the spoons and the ends of the handles.
4. Paint and finish surfaces as desired.
5. Mount a spoon at each end of the board, securing the bowl of the spoon to the top and the handle on the back with screws.
6. Press felt self-stick pads on the bottom. ❏

LADLE CANDLEHOLDER

A ladle makes an interesting wall sconce. Choose a candle that fits the size of the ladle. Created by Susan Goans Driggers

You'll Need:

A ladle	A rectangular wooden plaque
Acrylic paint	Paint brush
Antiquing stain	Drill with drill bits and screw attachment
Sandpaper	Screw
Tack cloth	Sawtooth hanger
Rag or sponge	A candle

Here's How:

1. Sand wooden surface smooth. Wipe away dust with a tack cloth.
2. Drill a hole in the ladle handle.
3. Paint the plaque with acrylic paint. Let dry.
4. Sand the plaque on the edges to expose the wood for a worn look. Wipe away dust.
5. Apply antiquing to the plaque with a rag or a sponge. Wipe away excess. Let dry.
6. Attach a sawtooth hanger to the back of the plaque.
7. Mount a ladle on board with a screw, using photo as a guide for placement. ❑

Metric Conversion Chart
INCHES TO MILLIMETERS AND CENTIMETERS

Inches	MM	CM		Yards	Meters
1/8	3	.3		1/8	.11
1/4	6	.6		1/4	.23
3/8	10	1.0		3/8	.34
1/2	13	1.3		1/2	.46
5/8	16	1.6		5/8	.57
3/4	19	1.9		3/4	.69
7/8	22	2.2		7/8	.80
1	25	2.5		1	.91
1-1/4	32	3.2		2	1.83
1-1/2	38	3.8		3	2.74
1-3/4	44	4.4		4	3.66
2	51	5.1		5	4.57
3	76	7.6		6	5.49
4	102	10.2		7	6.40
5	127	12.7		8	7.32
6	152	15.2		9	8.23
7	178	17.8		10	9.14
8	203	20.3			
9	229	22.9			
10	254	25.4			
11	279	27.9			
12	305	30.5			

Index